Table of Contents

Spiraling 2
Limbo 3
Fading 4
Through the Snow 5
Ambition 6
Command 7
Pieces 9
Sins Forgotten 11
The Girl That Sits Reading 13
Staring Into Nothing 16
Embers Die 17
Winter's Breath 19
Leftovers 21
Vines 22
The Beggar Child 23
Butterflies 26
Count to Ten 26
The Sisters 26
Human 26
Horrors 26
Like a Glove 28
Climax 28
Apologies 28
Mercy 28
Feast 28
Sleepless 30

Spiraling

Behind every corner
A shadow waiting with icy fingers

Every fluttering curtain
A harbinger of chaos to come

I step around the corners
Peel back the curtains

Always finding nothing
But the cold mocking silence

Still I keep my senses swiveling
Wondering of what is never there

Limbo

It's a waiting game
All of it
Each moment
Ticking through its inevitability

We never thought
This is where we would find it
In the spinning of a falling leaf
Carried by the fall breeze

In the slow waltz
Of dust dancing in sunbeams
In the silence
Of Sunday morning

Is this it?
We ask ourselves
Unable to understand
Satisfaction

Is this what we missed?
We wonder
Not knowing
How we should be feeling

No matter the milestones of life
We achieve
No matter the achievements
Unlock

Like flies struggling
In the spider's web
We remain stuck

Fading

It's a peculiar feeling
Nothingness approaching
The artist's eraser
Upon you

Hollow
Isn't quite the right word
Empty
Doesn't begin to describe

No, it's more of a fading
A slowly steady slipping
Of the person
You once were

Peace
Isn't quite the right word
Fear
Doesn't really describe

No, it's more like
The casual indifference
Of an observer
With no pieces left to play

The game ends

Through the Snow

He trudges
Convinced of his righteousness

Holding grudges
That crawl deeper into his bones

With each step

The lashes of frost
Numbing his limbs

The howling bites of ice
Freeze his streaking tears

There is no going back

He has become kin
With the abusive storm
That surrounds him

His eyes see only a white tunnel
Swirling out in front of him
All else has faded

So he keeps putting one foot
In front of the other
Head bent forward
Into the oncoming abuse

He is relentless
But so is the storm

Ambition

Down the hole
Plummeting
Faster
Faster
Faster still

One after another
Mistakes pile upon
Regrets become my closest friend
Keeping me warm and awake
On lonely nights

Intimacy of the highest order
With my own desires
Wants and lusts
Hungering forever unsatiated

Leapfrogging myself
Tumbling down the hill
Bones shattering against stones
Of my own creation
The bottom never drawing nearer

Sunrises turn to sunsets
Sunlight into starlight
The tides wax and wane
At the command of the moon
As the universe drifts by

But I just keep rolling
Ever downward
Trapped

Command

Her flesh is taught
Wound tightly over her bones
Stretched thin by fear and excitement

Her sight has been taken
Wrapped in a cool cloth
Of anticipation

Her wrists are bound
In cuffs of desire
Tied by her freedom

Candlelight flickers
Casting ghosts upon the walls
Reifying her fantasies

Violins sing in her head
Nothing else to be heard
She drifts into pleasure

She is warm
Wracked with tremors
At gentle touches

Her body rises
Of its own accord
To meet him

Thunder and lightning
Flame and smoke
The iciest chill

The rains pour
Marking the land

With the night's deeds

She is lost in the wilds
Trapped in her sins
In their beautiful wickedness

The night bows to her

Pieces

Shattered snowflakes
Sparkle in the moonlight
Decorating an unseen floor
Sunk into black

Bits of all I've lost
Broken like weak glass
Glisten and dance
Filling the night air

Memories
Of loves lost
Friendships forgotten
Hopes murdered

Like ballerinas dancing
Wishes and dreams
Float around
These pieces of me

It's a joyous scene
The revelry of demons
Taunting and laughing
Telling their story

I am on my knees
My breath is heavy
Shards of glass
Tear at my lungs

The moonlight makes silver rivers
Of tears streaming down my cheeks
The gasps of despair are hot
Painting the night with desperation

I grab each snowflake
Gently guiding them back together
Recreating what was once whole
In hopes of a rebirth

A wild wind whips in the darkness
Rending asunder
What I have glued back together
The facade of hope cracks and fades

The ballerinas cackle
Continue their dancing
Their mesmerizing drifting
On steel toes

A wail pierces the black
Parting my drying lips
A chill crawls unseen
In the unforgiving night

My fingers once again go to work
Sisyphus reborn
Here in the spiraling shadows
A slave feverishly works

Sins Forgotten

See the screaming of memories
As they disappear in the revery

This is where crimes are forgiven
Where lust is the only religion

Knots undone
Inhibitions unbecome

They are lost in each other
Flames of shame are smothered

Two are become
Transformed into one

Serpents tongues lash in the darkness
Seeking comfort in the other's caress

The strongest hunger bares its teeth
Burning away fear with its heat

Thirst that longs to be satiated
Want that cannot be abated

Too long has this moment stayed
Growing in its womb for too many days

Cries and moans
Grins and groans

The hours melt away
Dancing eyes ablaze

Crescendos echo through the air

Silent unheard prayers

Panting like animals they collapse
Lying in their own trap

Barriers crumble and demons return
The coals are all but burned
Embers die like stillborn babes
Having spent all they gave

Gravity pulls like an old friend
A force that never ends

Sins that were forgotten
Festering and rotten

Return with renewed strength
Desperate to breach the arm's length

They lie in each other's embrace
Trying to keep themselves safe

But under the hot breath
Begins a slow death

Mistakes have been made
Regrets created under the moon's shade

Such is the lovers' dance
A ballet of sickly romance

The Girl That Sits Reading

A hundred sleepless nights filled with fantastic dreams of fright
Led me to this crumbling ledge upon which I now stood
Jump from here and take flight into the unforgiving night
I had promised the phantoms in my head I would
To end my sorrows, to terminate this time I had borrowed, a vow that I would see no morrow

Such was the state I was in on that night when the haunting did begin
Beckoned by a sad twilight's unforgiving shadow
I was fraught with dark fluttering thoughts, and in that state I sought
Some respite from those thoughts I sought on the cobbles down below
Would I have imagined thoughts would become demons and I would relive a hundred sorrows

As I twitched that final step, a faint fluttering did echo
Behind me in my empty study as I sought to dash myself upon the cobbles down below
The faintest of flutterings, the lightest of flippings did echo
Carried by a prayer on the still air it reached me before I silenced the next tomorrow
Like the pages of a book flipping, the faint fluttering did echo

Arrested by the lilt of this new song, I felt weak where I had once felt strong
Such was the power of that brief beautiful flutter
For it took but that one sound, to entreat me to turn around
To make my first step stutter; And so I turned back into my empty study closing the shutters
There upon the armchair I had groomed with a thousand sittings she sat smiling, quietly flipping

Like the pages in her book, my heart was sent aflutter; At the site of this child I quietly muttered

"By the Lord," such was my entreaty, "do my distressed eyes now deceive me?"
A life of nightmares had not brought before me, such a horror as this spectre looking toward me
In those smiling eyes I saw a memory, fluttering like the pages of her book of story
Of what I had loved and killed; the thorns of memory began pricking, as she sat quietly flipping

"Dear girl, who are you?" my voice strained and hoarse, "Tell me, who are you?"
"Did you come from some far away shore? From what demon or angel were you born?"
I stood silently waiting, the last threads of my sanity slowly fading
There was no answer, no retort to my desperate call; It seemed she had not heard me at all
Upon my own words I began faltering; upon my own thoughts I began tripping

"Tell me child. Have you come to settle the score? For those sins I have committed before?"
Still no answer, no respite for my curious wondering; I kept diving, continued my blundering
"Tell me, tell me I implore! Are you the recompense for what I have wrought before?"
Nothing greeted my thundering; nothing but the cold unfeeling flipping answered my wondering
But of course I already knew, this demon had come to bring life to my nightmares anew
No lord in Heaven, nor devil in Hell, has answered my call
So still she sits in that armchair that had once been mine
And still no sleep will come to still my spiraling mind
The window remains shuttered, and my hands remain still
I continue to hear the cobbles calling from below the window sill

There is now no respite to be found, no escape from that fluttering sounds
Here am I lost in my own memories, of murder and death I caused so cleverly
Haunted by this spectre of my own creation, sitting in that chair each time I turn around
She sits reading neverendingly, flipping her pages and smiling in her revelry
Never answering, never speaking, she just sits, quietly flipping

Staring Into Nothing

He sinks
Staring into the black
No, not quite black
Because black would be something
He could identify black
Could attach himself to it
Could feel some familiarity with it

He may even speak to it
In a language they both understand
A language of darkness and shadows
Of death and decay
Whispers and secrets
Crimes and sins
But no such luck
For his is not such fortune
To have a world which he knows
A friend he can hold

So he sits sinking
Into the ever present nothing
An emptiness so absolute
It defies words
Even nothing is not suitable
To describe the what
Or more accurately the lack of what
That stares back at him

He smiles
For he knows
He is become

Embers Die

Fluttering sparks
Like butterflies flitting
Back and forth
Dance and disappear
In his mind's eye

Little lightning bugs
Jittering and blinking
Against a backdrop
Of unseen crickets chirping
Chirping their eternal song

They die, these bugs
These butterflies don't live long
In life or in memory
The briefest of flickers
Burning stars

That's all that's left of her
Of her shine
As bright as the sun it was
Burning too brightly
Burning itself out

He lies almost still
Save for one frail hand
That brushes silver threads
Hanging just barely so
From a skull just years from dust

The embers may burn and die
But so long as she is with him
By his side
In their bed

They will light again

If only for moments
Pinpricks in the night sky
They will light again
They embers will burn
So long as she is with him

Winter's Breath

He breathes deep
Filling his lungs
With the icy chill
Of a wolf's hunger

Everything but this moment
Is forgotten
He lives in the now
Welcoming the frost

His motions are fluid
But commanding
The control is intoxicating
The frozen liquor works its way into him

His palm slides up her body
Tense with desire unhinged
His fingers close lightly
Ever so lightly, around her neck

A moan drifts into the night
Imperceptible outside of their embrace
As she arches
To meet his thrusts

Her eyes are bluer than ever before
The winter has breathed life into them
They sparkle and dance oceans of wanting
The huntress inside her looks upon life

She digs icicles into him
Pulling with the coldest desperation
Drawing him into her
The icy storm rises

The chill grows like a tree's roots
A spiraling spider web
Sinking deep into them
Awakening parts of them long asleep

Gunshots echo as the shutters slam
But they are deaf
Branches shatter and fall by them
But they are blind to the destruction

Winter breathes its most violent breath
Whipping the night like a master
Punishing its slaves
But the slaves have found freedom
Lost in their lust

The blizzard howls
As the pair crescendo
Hot panting melting the frost
Tremors wracking tense bodies

The wind dies down
Snowflakes drift exhausted to the ground
The last echos of the master's whip
Reverberates in the stillness

Smiles glistening under the waning moon
They collapse
Into a tangle of heavy breathing
A sweaty mess of pleased sighs

Leftovers

Dinners uneaten
Rotting in the freezer
Dust settling on peeling bannisters
Cracks webbing through weak glass

Years the house has lain
Dormant and undisturbed
Home only to ghosts unseen
Unheard by any

A crimson rug of blood
Lays dried on the kitchen tiles
Darkness seeped into it
The bright red turned the color of shadow

Grey listless eyes
Three pairs
Stare into the silence
Father, mother, and child

None believed their cries
None heard their calls
Save for the demons
Who took them

The tragedy of not being believed
Paints the pretties scene
On a canvas devoid of life
Trapped in a haunting moment

Vines

All shades of green
Swaying slightly
In the light caress of the wind
Clinging with gentle fingers

They spent their lives crawling
Never walking
Never running
Forever crawling

Gaia's fingers reach upward
Searching for the sky
Spreading life
Or trying anyway

Limits unsurmountable
Life stifled
Mother Earth fails herself
Her reach only goes so far

The Beggar Child

Walking along my thoughts drifting
The sands of my mind ever shifting

I was returned to that morning
When the rain began pouring

The spring's herald of a new birth
Quenching the thirst of the earth

In a rush a began running
To escape my thoughts were turning

When right in front of me
Stood a child not four foot three

Dirt staining his pallid face
Empty eyes staring from their place

The water came down stronger
I wished to stay out no longer

Not ten steps farther had a run
When once again that child stood in front

"What do you want of me?"
I asked uncertainly

He just kept looking in the wet morning air
Silently tilting his head to quizzically stare

A cold grin spread across his cheeks
As the morning grew ever more bleak

He held out a tiny hand

I was stunned by a gesture so grand

Growing more sudden ever the while
I searched for something to give the child

"Sorry," I said sullenly
"I have nothing. You came so suddenly."
The smile quickly thawed
And turned to a black gaping maw

His eyes so innocent and cool
Transformed into deep black pools

Suddenly I was drowning in shadow
By darkness I had been swallowed

All my sins thus laid bare
In front of me my crimes declared

Such terror I had never felt
Fear taking me I fell to my knees and knelt

Tears streaming down my hot cheeks
Begging forgiveness but unable to speak

I begged and begged and begged
Only by that unending dark was I greeted

As suddenly as it had come
The storm was then undone

To that morning I was returned
Darkness disappearing as it had begun

I spun wildly searching for that child
But saw no sight of that gaping smile

My heart calmed slowly and settled
I gathered my resolve and mettle

I rose from knees
Marveling that I had been let free

I looked up at the sky
Realizing I was completely dry

I could do nothing then but cry

Butterflies

The chrysalides crack
Lightning breaking across the shells
They are born fangs bared
Wings unfurled they take flight
Rising into the sun

Count to Ten

Let the heat simmer
Let the storm settle
Let the thunder rest
Let the lightning flash
Count it down

The Sisters

Destinies hang on their command
They whisper plans to each other
Pulling their puppeteer's strings
Commanding us like marionettes
We dance at their whims

Human

I am only human
But hold the weight of expectations
Fit only for a god
My resolve crumbles
I am brought to my knees

Horrors

Unbidden they come
Every night under shadow

Every morning under blinding light
There is no hiding
From the horrors that haunt me

Like a Glove

She fits perfectly
Every curve, every contour
Like puzzle pieces we join
I am held warmly
As if resting inside a glove

Climax

The hot sliding of flesh on flesh
Burning breath on sweaty brows
Heaving chests, twisting heaps
The moans grow louder and louder
Until silenced by the perfect moment

Apologies

Hollow words
Falling on deaf ears
They ring like bells
Tolling from crumbling towers
Worthless words

Mercy

I beg forgiveness
Neigh, respite
From the interminable scratching
That never ceases
Behind these eyes

Feast

Their cries of pain

Their final begging
That last whisper of breath
The final acceptance
Such a beautiful buffet

Sleepless

Here I sit surrounded by all the trappings
Everything I have ever desired
Lost in everything I have collected
Possessions unlike any you have seen

Mine, it is all mine
Each little thing belongs to me

Possessions, though, are not enough to
Let me sleep soundly
Each hour passes more slowly
Serpentining into the next
Every moment bleeds gradually in the night

How have I become
Each person I sought to destroy
Left undone by my own hand
Parted with my soul long ago

My life drifts by in this darkness
Ever sleepless and tired I drown

Made in the USA
Columbia, SC
08 December 2022